Peaceful Community Pocket Guide

PREVENT LIFESPAN BULLYING & IMPROVE SOCIAL CLIMATE

by K.P. Cardinal, M.S.

Digital & Print

Peaceful Community Pocket Guide

PREVENT LIFESPAN BULLYING & IMPROVE SOCIAL CLIMATE

Published by K.P. Cardinal
via Createspace
and KDP

ISBN-13: 978-1539177067
ISBN-10: 1539177068

Peaceful
Community
Pocket Guide
K.P. Cardinal

How to Use this Book

Read cover to cover or one page per day.
Educate people of all ages on social wellness.
Attach a tip to your cubicle or door at work.
Print/screenshot pages and display in the community.
Work the lessons into continuing education for staff.
Have as part of a presentation / teaching tool.
Attach reminders to your mirror.
Talk to young children about peaceful communities.
Use as part of a meditation, prayer or support group.
Spread the message on social media.
Email to a friend or colleague.
Weave into life to make the world better.

An unhealthy social climate
is present when unkindness,
bullying and other forms
of social aggression
go unstopped or are not
identified as harmful.

Social wellness
and social illness
cannot exist
in the same
moment.

Contribute to the positive climate in your community by contributing peace to each moment.

Our body
instinctively
knows the difference
between illness
and wellness.

In social settings, stop and listen to what your body is telling you.

We have to learn
social wellness
basics to know when
social illness threatens
the emotional climate
in a community.

To fully understand social wellness, it is helpful to learn about social illness and compare how we feel in different environments.

Bullying,
another term
for social illness
or social aggression,
is at the opposite end
of the spectrum from
positive social climate.

We have to realize that bullying, at its base, is about abuse of power, discrimination, and bigotry.

-Rosalind Wiseman
Thought Leader & School Bullying Expert

Relational aggression
(also known as bullying)
is a lifelong phenomenon
found in every
socioeconomic class
and in every culture.

Bullying is a lifespan issue.
People can be targets
of bullying or engage
in bullying at any age.

A bully may attempt to bully anyone. However, their efforts end up being most effective against those with less power and less resources. They may act their worst privately with vulnerable people, then publically display a more likeable side of themselves.

Mediation does not typically solve problems between a bully and target because of a power imbalance.
It is not advised for bullies and targets to “talk it out” with a mediator. A target may be further victimized.

It is a myth that aggressive talk is “just talk” and has no damaging consequences. Words contribute to and often set the stage for physical assault and violence.

It's important for
people who have power
to model social wellness by
treating others with dignity
and demonstrating a
capacity for empathy.

When witnessing
leaders, observe
their behaviors and style.
See if you can sense
on a visceral level
if social illness
or social wellness
is at play.

When witnessing
groups of people
in community settings,
observe whether
social illness
or social wellness
is at play.

It is important for
a group that has power
to not give power
to individuals inclined
to misuse their power
in ways that promote
social aggression.

There are 4 main options
in a bully drama:
1)Align with the Bully
2)Align with the Target
(best to do with support)
3)Act as a Silent Bystander
4)Act as an Upstander
for positive social
benefit

Option 1

Align with Bully

You value what the bully stands for. You actively or passively support them—not a role of integrity.

Option 2
Align with Target

You have empathy for the target.
Warning— if you actively
support a target and don't have power,
you risk becoming a target.
Align with leaders that
match a bully's power.

Option 3
Witnesses & Bystanders

You see what's happening but,
because you sense risk,
you choose to remain silent
in an effort to preserve yourself.
You feel powerless.

Option 4
Leaders / Upstanders

Only empathetic leaders with power, and those fully supported by them, can safely act as upstanders against a bully or bully posse. A critical mass in a community must play this role for social wellness to prevail.

The best leaders
have empathy and
a history of using their
power for the good of others,
even those different from
themselves.

Empathy:
The feeling that you understand and share another person's experiences and emotions.

Merriam –Webster Dictionary

It may be easier
to understand people similar to us.
However, being able to put ourselves in
another's shoes, with empathy,
contributes to a healthy social climate
within communities.
Positive leaders have a
distinct capacity for empathy.

Being open to someone different from yourself (practicing social wellness) means you're less likely to judge a person or put them down for their differences.

Some people say older people are less likely to change and are more likely to be close minded. That's not true. Believing that is a form of ageism.

Racism is
a form of social illness
exhibited when
a person feels and acts
in ways consistent with the
misguided belief that their
race is superior.

Sexism is
a form of social illness
exhibited when
a person feels and acts
in ways consistent with the
misguided belief that their
gender is superior.

Xenophobia is
a form of social illness
exhibited when a person
feels intense or irrational
dislike or fear of people
from other countries.

Religious discrimination involves treating a person unfavorably because of their religious beliefs. Ironically, some who now discriminate based on religious beliefs have ancestors who sought religious freedom, and suffered or died because of faith.

Be an LGBTQ Upstander

Homophobia and transphobia create an environment in which LGBTQ individuals may have to face harassment and even violence in schools, communities and/or homes.

Gay Straight Alliance Network, San Francisco, CA

Unfortunately, some individuals grow up in a climate of social illness. This explains why there are people in the world who dislike others simply because they are different.

If we were once taught
to fear or dislike others
different from ourselves,
we can change
this thought pattern
by getting to know
people and seeking
common ground.

A person who is
inclined to bully,
can be rich or poor,
young or old, tall, short,
have any skin color
and be from anywhere
on earth.

A person who
displays and promotes
civility and kindness
can be rich or poor,
young or old, tall, short,
have any skin color
and be from anywhere
on earth.

A person who bullies
can be from any
political party
or espouse
any set of beliefs.

Part of a bully's tactics
may be to label those who
stand up to them,
calling them a bully in return.
Shifting the focus is a strategy
that may fool some,
but not all. Don't be fooled.

A social aggressor may appear to have many friends, be well-liked, even be popular and may claim to speak on behalf of many. It’s a myth that bullies are viewed as unpopular.

The group
who gives a person
who bullies further power,
is fueling social illness.
This makes matters
worse, especially for those
who are potential targets
of bullying.

Bullying thrives
in communities when individuals
do not speak up because
they lack power and are not
supported by those with power.

Desire to be
“politically correct”
is simply
a desire to be kind.

When one chooses the opposite of political correctness, it is often unkind, disrespectful and either comes from a place of misguided ignorance, or is deliberately intended to cause harm. An innocent faux pas may be forgiven with a sincere apology. However, knowingly attempting to cause harm contributes to poor social climate.

Some words and phrases deemed “not politically correct” are considered as such because they are associated with violence perpetrated against a group simply because of their differences. Certain words can trigger emotional pain for individuals of a certain ethnicity, religious background or sexual orientation.

Behavioral contagion
is a type of social influence.
It is when certain behaviors
exhibited by one person
are copied by others who are either
in the vicinity of the original actor,
or have been exposed to
media coverage describing
the behavior of the
original actor.

When a
bully becomes
powerful and wins
over followers,
that is when
social wellness
is most
threatened.

Bullying must be
identified as a significant
lifespan problem
worthy of understanding
so that our most vulnerable
citizens, likely targets,
do not suffer.

Likely targets
of bullying are weaker,
more vulnerable
marginalized people:
elders, children and those
emotionally, physically and
economically challenged.

The key to managing social aggression within communities is found in the education, training and modeling of civil behavior in our workers, human resource professionals, teachers, parents, clergy and world leaders at the top of hierarchies.

If the leadership
isn’t onboard with wanting
to create a culture
of dignity within
any organization,
it isn’t likely to happen.

Donna Hicks – Harvard University

Just as parents and teachers require coaching from experts on bullying among children, so do people in all organizations within living and working communities.

An individual is considered a target of bullying when exposed repeatedly over time to negative actions with intent to harm on the part of one or more other people. These actions can be physical, verbal or relational in nature.

Bonifas & Frankel 2012, Olweus 2015

An individual or group is less likely to get support in a bullying situation if the bully or bullies succeed in keeping that person or group isolated from those who can defend them.

Cyber bullying is considered bullying and occurs via technology through texts, emails or online social networks.

Dilmac, 2009, msisac.cisecurity.org, 2015

Bullying behaviors can include:
Intentional emotional or physical injury,
aggressive actions or words spoken
directly to a person or behind a person's back;
making mean faces or gestures,
spreading rumors or untruths,
and intentionally excluding someone.

Robin Bonifas, 2016

Conflict vs. Bullying

Bullying is different from conflict.
Conflict is a disagreement or argument
in which both sides express their views.
Bullying is negative behavior
directed by someone exerting
power and control over another person.

pacer.org

Verbal bullying
involves name calling, teasing
insults, taunts, threats,
sarcasm, or pointed jokes
targeting specific individuals.

Robin Bonifas, 2014

Physical bullying
can include pushing, hitting,
destroying property
or stealing.

Robin Bonifas, 2014

Socially aggressive bullying includes shunning, excluding, gossiping, spreading rumors and using negative, non-verbal body language, such as mimicking or offensive gestures.

Robin Bonifas, 2014

Individuals who witness bullying report being harmed as well.
They often experience negative emotions, just as victims do.

Robin Bonifas, 2014

People suffering
with forms of dementia
or certain medical and
emotional conditions
may act in ways that look
exactly like bullying.
This is not the same.
Consult a professional.

Some people exhibit verbal or physical aggression when they are frustrated or upset as a way of communicating their feelings. This is not necessarily bullying.

Robin Bonifas, 2014

Bullies may
use deceptive and hurtful
methods to isolate their targets
from others so that
they feel afraid and alone.
They may make up lies
and also may pre-emptively
call others liars
to gain control and have
the upper hand.

Bullying
often
hides
in
plain
sight.

Sit Together

“If no one sits near a
particular child
in the school cafeteria,
all the classmates are the bullies
yet the victim cannot confront
the ringleader.”

- Kathleen Stassen Berger, 2007

Be Kind.
There are countless documented
incidents in all age groups
where social aggression
has contributed to
anxiety, depression,
physical pain and even
homicide and suicide.

Social aggression hurts individuals and communities. Let us all focus on how each of us can improve the social and emotional climate in living and working environments.

Be safe by
getting adequate
support, professional or
otherwise, and use
your own voice
as an upstander
when you see or hear
someone harming
another.

Don’t laugh
when an offensive joke
is told at the
expense of another,
even if the person
is not present.

Malicious teasing is either hurtful and public or when a person is teased for their insecurities and is labeled "uptight" and "too sensitive".

- Rosalind Wiseman

If you have been
a target of bullying,
it’s not about you.
A bully will find a new
and different target
if you are not there.
It’s about them.

When visiting a new place, learn the culturally accepted way to say “hello”. Learn about different traditions and customs throughout the world.

One human right
which is part of the
1948 Universal Declaration of
Human Rights
is that people have
a right to equality.

When you judge someone's appearance, notice that your mind begins to evaluate the other, and stop. Open the mind to allowing others the dignity of being who they are.

Notice the beauty and musical cadence in all of the world's languages. View accents and variations in speech as part of what makes a person who they are– a valuable and unique individual.

People with disabilities have rights.
Be considerate toward individuals
as they navigate the world with
a service dog, cane, walker or wheelchair.

Those with disabilities are human beings with feelings. Recognize that under different circumstances that person could be you.

"There, but for the grace of God, go I."

- John Bradford, 16th century

Seeing yourself as
better, surrounded by those
you see as less than,
does not make it so.
See others as equals.

For Leaders:

Listen and let
your community coach you.
If you hear that bullying
exists but you don't see it
directly, believe it's there
and ask more questions.

The Goal:

A critical mass of social wellness is necessary for people to feel emotional safety on a visceral level within a community. It's how the most vulnerable people feel that counts.

When social wellness, or social climate is enhanced, life is better for all individuals within the community, not just those aligned with the powerful.

Emotional and physical safety and sense of belonging are essential to our highest potential.

Abraham Maslow

Peaceful
Community
Pocket Guide
K.P. Cardinal

Maslow's Hierarchy of Needs

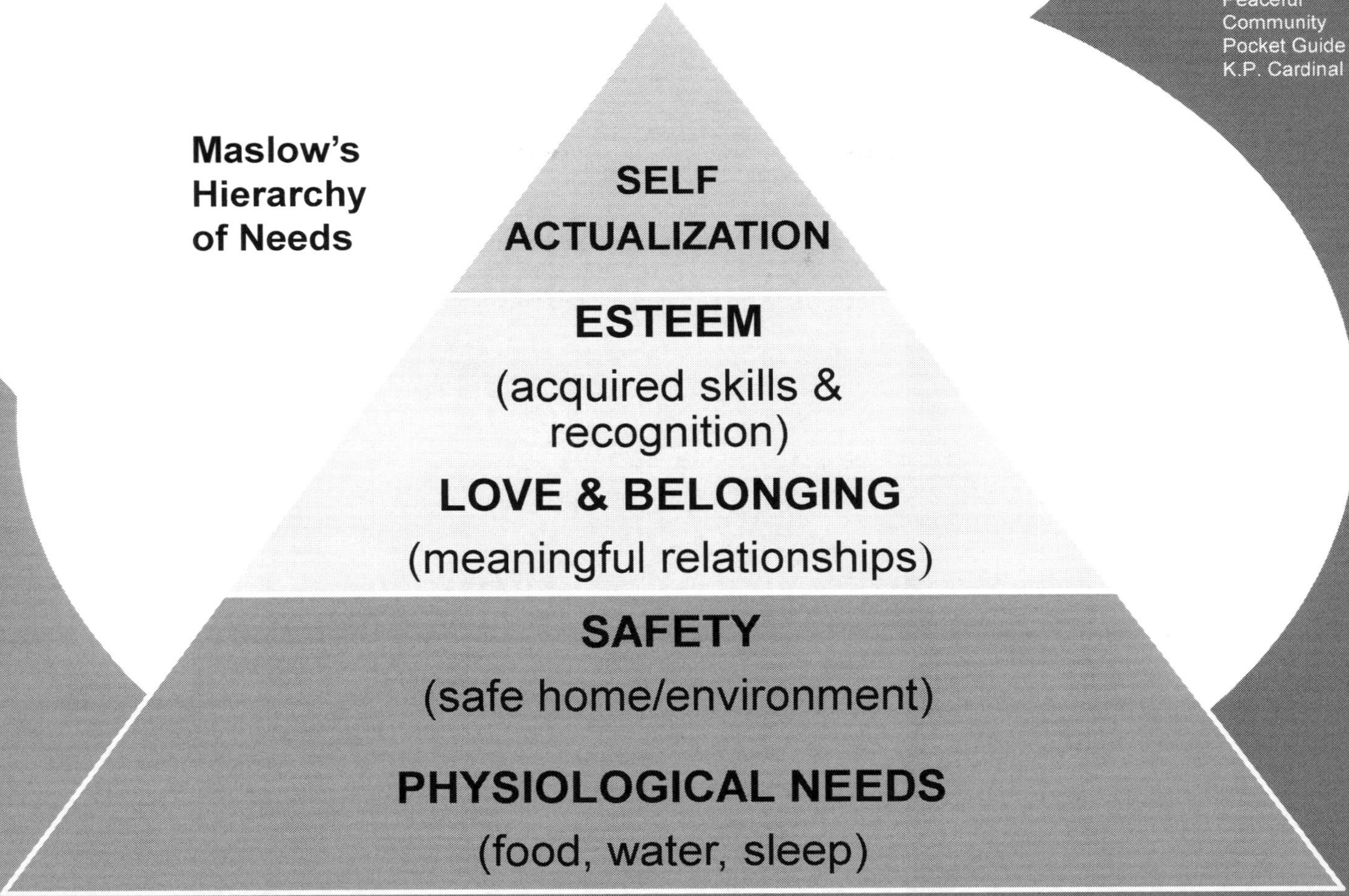

SELF ACTUALIZATION

ESTEEM

(acquired skills & recognition)

LOVE & BELONGING

(meaningful relationships)

SAFETY

(safe home/environment)

PHYSIOLOGICAL NEEDS

(food, water, sleep)

Anti-bullying is aligned with
The Golden Rule
"Do Unto Others"
which is found
in many of the
world's great religions.

“Do unto others”

Christianity

All things whatsoever ye would that men should do to you, do ye so to them; for this is the law and the prophets.

The Bible; Matthew 7:1

“Do unto others”

Confucianism

Do not do to others what you would not like yourself. Then there will be no resentment against you, either in the family or in the state.

Analects 12:2

“Do unto others”

Buddhism

Hurt not others in ways that you yourself would find hurtful.

Udana-Varga

“Do unto others”

Hinduism

This is the sum of duty; do naught unto others what you would not have them do unto you.

Mahabharata 5,1517

“Do unto others”

Islam

No one of you is a believer until he desires for his brother that which he desires for himself.

Sunnah

"Do unto others"

Judaism

What is hateful to you, do not do to your fellowman. This is the entire law; all the rest is commentary.

Talmud, Shabbat

“Do unto others”

Taoism

Regard your neighbor’s gain as your gain, and your neighbor’s loss as your own loss.

Tai Shang Kan Yin P’ien

Be Kind.
for everyone you meet
is fighting a battle you
know nothing about.

Updated version of Plato by Wendy Mass

We must become
the change we want to see.

- Mahatma Gandhi

References

Berger, K.S. (2007) Update on bullying at school: Science forgotten. Developmental Review, 27, 90-126.

Bonifas, R. and Frankel, M. (2012, Feb. 8) Senior Bullying: Guest Post by Robin Bonifas, PhD, MSW, and Marsha Frankel, LICSW retrieved on March 28, 2015 from mybetternursinghome.com

Bonifas, Robin (2014, April 22) Recognizing and Curtailing Bullying Among Older Adults, Power point presented at the 17th Anniversary Arizona ALFA Spring Conference and Trade Show

Briles, Judith (2009) Stabotage! How to Deal with the Pit Bulls, Skunks, Snakes, Scorpions & Slugs in the Health Care Workplace, The Briles Group, Inc.

Dilmac, Bulent (2009) Psychological Needs as a Predictor of Cyber bullying: a Preliminary Report on College Students, Educational Sciences: Theory & Practice, 9 (3) pp. 1308-1320.

Farrington, David P. (1993) Understanding and Preventing Bullying. The University of Chicago Press, Crime and Justice, Vol. 17 (1993), pp. 381-458

Hamburger ME, Basile KC, Vivolo AM. (2011) Measuring Bullying Victimization, Perpetration, and Bystander Experiences: A Compendium of Assessment Tools. Atlanta, GA: Centers for Disease Control and Prevention, National Center for Injury Prevention and Control retrieved on April 7, 2015 from http://www.cdc.gov/violenceprevention/pdf/BullyCompendiumBk-a.pdf

Knauer, Nancy J. (2009) LGBT Elder Law: Toward Equity in Aging. Harvard Journal of Law and Gender, Vol. 32, 2009, pp.302-358.

Kreimer, Susan (2012) “Older Adults Can Be Bullies, Too-- Seniors in nursing homes, assisted living facilities face peer pressure from other seniors” AARP Bulletin, March 2012 retrieved on January 16, 2015 at www.aarp.org/relationships/friends-family/info-03-2012/older-adults-can-be-bullies-too

Lake, Neil (2014, November 14) Bullying Is Ageless: Conflict and Violence Widespread In Nursing Homes, Study Finds, WBUR’s Common Health: Reform and Reality (November 14, 2014)

Laugeson, Elizabeth and Frankel, Fred (2014, December 12). UCLA Peers Clinic, Retrieved on March 22, 2015 from http://www.semel.ucla.edu/peers

Maslow, K., and Ory, M. (2001). Review of a Decade of Dementia Special Care Unit Research: Lessons Learned and Future Directions. Alzheimer’s Care Quarterly, 2, 3, 10-16.

Olweus Bullying Prevention Program (2015) Hazelden Foundation retrieved on March 22, 2015 at hazelden.org/olweus

Olweus, D. (1978) Aggression in schools. Washington, DC: Hemisphere.

Olweus, D. (1993) Bullying at school: What we know and what we can do. Cambridge, MA: Blackwell.

Olweus, D, Ed. J. Juvonen and S. Graham (2001) "Peer Harassment: A Critical Analysis and Some Important Issues," in Peer Harassment in School Guilford Publications, NY 3-20

Olweus, D. (2003) A profile of bullying at school. Educational Leadership, 60(6), 12-17.

Pacer Center, Inc. (2012) Action Sheet BP-18, Bullying and Harassment of Students with Disabilities: Top 10 facts parents, educators, and students need to know, retrieved on March 29, 2015 from http://www.pacer.org/bullying/resources/students-with-disabilities/

Polanin, Joshua R., Espelage, Dorothy L., Pigott, Therese D. (2012) A Meta-Analysis of School-Based Bullying Prevention Programs' on Bystander Intervention Behavior, School Psychology Review, 41(1) pp.47-65

Raskind, Murray A. (1999) Evaluation and management of aggressive behavior in the elderly demented patient. The Journal of Clinical Psychiatry 60 Supp. 15:45-49

Rosen, T., Pillemer, K., & Lachs, M. (2008). Resident-to-Resident Aggression in Long-Term Care Facilities: An Understudied Problem. Aggression and Violent Behavior, 13(2), 77-78.

Span, Paula (2014, November 25) Aggressive Neighbors in the Nursing Home. The New York Times Salmivalli, K. Lagerspetz, K. Björkqvist, K. Osterman, and A. Kaukiainen (1996) "Bullying as a Group Process: Participant Roles and Their Relations to Social Status within the Group," Aggressive Behavior (22) 1-15.

Shepherd, Shawna (2011, March 10) White House Conference Tackles Bullying, CNN retrieved on April 27, 2015 at http://www.cnn.com/2011/POLITICS/03/10/obama.bullying

Tilly, Jane and Reed, Peter (2004) Evidence on Interventions to Improve Quality of Care for Residents with Dementia in Nursing and Assisted Living Facilities, The Alzheimer's Association

Tokunaga, Robert S. (2010) Following you home from school: A critical review and synthesis of research on cyberbullying victimization, Computers in Human Behavior (26) 3, pp.277-287

Trumpetter, H., Scholte, R. and Westerhof, G. (2010) Resident-to-resident relational aggression and subjective well-being in assisted living facilities. Aging & Mental Health, 15, 59-67

Valliancourt, T. (2005) Indirect aggression among humans. In R.E. Tremblay, W.W. Hartup, & J. Archer, Developmental origins of aggression (pp.158-177). New York: Guilford Press.

Voyer P, (2005) Prevalence of physical and verbal aggression behaviors and associated factors among older adults in long-term care facilities. BMC Geriatrics 5:13

Weiner, Jennifer (2015, January 17). Mean Girls in the Retirement Home, the New York Times, Sunday Review

Wiseman, R. (2002). Queen Bees and Wannabes. New York: Crown. Copyright 2003 Dan Olweus

Wood, F. (2007) Bullying in nursing homes: prevalence and consequences to psychological health. Dissertation Abstracts International, Volume: 68-05, Section: B, page: 3415.Thesis Ph.D. Walden University, 2007.

Workplace Bullying Institute (2014) Who We Are, retrieved on April 27 from http://www.workplacebullying.org/the-drs-namie

About the Author

Katherine has a master's degree in management of aging services from the John W. McCormack Graduate School of Policy and Global Studies, University of Massachusetts, Boston. Prior to becoming a gerontologist, she worked with adolescents challenged by histories of trauma and abuse. She received the 2015 Management of Aging Services Capstone Award highlighting how evidence-based school bullying prevention and intervention has application in aging services. Her work demonstrates how community leaders must view emotional climate as a responsibility within their power of influence. Synthesizing information across various disciplines, she invites social scientists to study links between social bullying and physical aggression and explore the complex nature of bullying that co-occurs with emotional/spiritual abuse, mental illness, substance abuse and forms of racism, homophobia, sexism and bigotry. Katherine presented findings from her capstone project (link below) at the 2016 Leading Age Wisconsin Spring Conference. She is a contributing author to the book, *Bullying Among Older Adults- How to Recognize and Address an Unseen Epidemic* by Robin P. Bonifas. Link to UMass Boston award winning capstone project: www.umb.edu/academics/mgs/gerontology/graduate/mgt_agingservices_ms/capstone_papers

Dedication

I wish to acknowledge family, friends and professionals who encouraged me on the journey that led to this publication, the capstone project, and becoming a contributing author for *Bullying Among Older Adults- How to Recognize and Address an Unseen Epidemic* by Dr. Robin Bonifas. Thank you for your time, insight, editorial comments and support Pamela Atwood, MS, Mary C. Butler, Robin Bonifas, PhD, Martin A. Donlan, Esq, Megan Eddy, MM, Beth Gershuny, PhD, Renee Gold, MS, Marguerite C. Rodney, M.Phil., Randi S. Thureson, University of Massachusetts, Boston professors Joan Hyde, PhD and Dan O'Leary, MA, my parents, husband, and daughter.

- KP Cardinal

Made in the USA
Columbia, SC
29 May 2017